The Amazon Seller:
How to Make Over $30,000
Per Month With Amazon FBA by
Optimizing Your Product Listing

by Chris Jones,
Founder & Chairman at ZonLife Success
Author of 12 Steps To Amazon Success

&

by Ben Gothard,
Founder & CEO of Gothard Enterprises LLC
Author of CEO at 20: A Little Book for Big Dreams

The Amazon Seller

Sales snapshot taken at 20 November 2016 22:34:44 GMT

Total order items	Units ordered	Ordered product sales	Avg. units/order item	Avg. sales/order item
22,126	**24,959**	**£290,752.45**	**1.13**	**£13.14**

Compare sales

Snapshot of Chris' past year selling on Amazon. £290,752.45 is roughly $365,606.67, which is about $30,467.22 per month.

Let's cut right to the chase. You want to learn how you can leverage Amazon in order to make an extra $30,000+ per month, and I don't blame you. Bringing in an additional six figures every single year could do a lot for most people. With that amount of income, financial stress can be turned into financial freedom. You wouldn't be worrying about whether or not you could pay the bills or waiting for that next paycheck to come in. Let's face it; an extra $30,000 per month would be life changing.

The issue that most people face when they are in financial need is not a lack of effort – there are plenty of people who put in 12 – 14 hour days and barely have enough money to put food on the table. The issue is that the effort they are putting in is helping somebody else get rich! As entrepreneur Jason Nazar says, "effort is relative." The same 12 – 14 hours per day that you spend slaving away for somebody else is the exact same work that it will take to build a business of your own that will pay you dividends for the rest of your, your children's, and possibly even your grandchildren's lives. The point I'm trying to make is that you need to own your own business in order to become financially free. As Robert Kiyosaki, author of *Rich Dad Poor Dad*, says, "Take responsibility for your finances—or get used to taking orders for the rest of your life. You're either a master of money or a slave to it. Your choice."

The question, then, is not why you should want to make an extra $30,000+ per month, but how you are going to do it. The old formula for success: go to school, study hard, and get good grades so you can get a good job, is just that – OLD! The only way to achieve true financial freedom is to create it. You control your own future only when you are in charge of your income source. You need your own business.

There are plenty of business models out there that can work. You could build hotels, buy a franchise, or even start a service-based business. The issue with all of these routes is that a lot of them take a significant amount of money, a lot of time and a sizeable team in order to start paying dividends. Amazon FBA, however, does not. You can start making money from this business model almost immediately from anywhere around the world (internet + laptop) without a lot of money or a team. Don't get me wrong; this business is not for the faint of heart. You are going to have to work really hard in order to see the results. There may even be times when you are tempted to give up. But, if you can put in the effort to build up your business, you will be able to make passive income on autopilot. Here's a little secret – $30,000 is only the beginning. In this book, Chris and I are going to share with you a proven step-by-step method to reaching the $30,000 a month benchmark, but the journey does not stop there. Once you've read through The Amazon Seller, you will see how Chris and I have put together a roadmap for you to be able to comfortably retire in 3 – 5 years. Read on to find out how.

Chris and I have been on two separate entrepreneurial paths for a few years now. He has been dominating Amazon FBA, writing books, blogging, and coaching people with the aim of helping them build financial freedom for themselves. I have been building my Social Media Marketing company, writing books, coaching people, and assembling masterminds of entrepreneurs who are far smarter than I am in order to channel their wisdom and help others achieve success in their personal and professional lives. Recently, after interviewing Chris for one of my masterminds, we found common ground in helping others become successful in their professional lives by becoming financially free. With Chris's experience in and unending success with ecommerce (specifically Amazon FBA), and my experience and credentials with Internet marketing (including Amazon), we decided to craft The Amazon Seller for you. In this definitive guide, we are going to lay out a pathway to success through Amazon FBA so that you too can make over $30,000 per month selling on Amazon and eventually retire in 3 – 5 years.

This book is going to approach the subject conversationally: I'm going to be asking Chris questions and we'll go back and forth until we've covered each aspect of this process. The four highlights of this piece include perfecting your Amazon listing, optimizing your Amazon Pay-Per-Click (PPC) to drive targeted traffic to your product listing, selecting the correct keywords for your product to show up on top of Amazon's search engine, and generating high quality, unbiased product reviews. By dominating these four aspects of Amazon, you will be able to generate over $30,000 per month within a short amount of time.

Before we jump into the technical side of things, I want to explore Chris' background so that you can have confidence that the advice we are passing along to you is sound.

Chris: I actually started out as a personal trainer many years ago. I got into fitness at about 18 years old because I've always wanted to help somebody else. I didn't just wanna work by myself, I wanted to help bring about a transformation in somebody else's life. I was a personal trainer in local gyms around Wales and the UK. I gave this path about 3 – 5 years and built up a good local reputation. However, I found myself working at least 12 – 16 hours a day at a wage that at first was okay, but couldn't sustain me forever. I eventually wanted to move to a bigger place, get a new car, etc., and it was not financially or time viable to stay where I was. I think everyone goes through this realization at a certain stage in his or her lives. One night I came home from my shift at the gym. I was covered in sweat from a 12 hour grind, had to go back to work in 6 hours, and wouldn't be able to take a day off in 4 more days. I though to myself, how long could I do this for?

I went home that night and typed in "how to make money while I sleep." That process then opened up an entirely new world to me. At first I dabbled in Self Publishing; I would pay somebody to write a book for me on a topic that I thought would sell, then I would publish it through Amazon Kindle Direct Publishing. I didn't have a clue what this was, but I knew that it was a possible route to earn the passive income that most people dream of. At first I didn't see much success, but after I started making a couple hundred pounds (UK) per month from selling books that I hadn't written myself, it came alive much more. I knew that this could be a very viable process that could serve me well into the long term.

Months went on and I continued selling on Kindle. It was pretty consistent, but then I came across Amazon FBA. This business model blew my mind. Essentially I could create my own branded products (Private Label) and sell those brands on Amazon myself in a fully automated process 24 hours a day, 7 days a week, 365 days a year. I could just sit back on my laptop and let my products do the work for me. Robert Kiyosaki always talks about making your money word hard for you, not the other way around. This was the closest thing I could find to this, so I immersed myself completely into Amazon FBA.

I wanted to become the master, so I self-taught myself for many months on the subject. Before I started my Amazon FBA journey, I literally locked myself in my room in my grandparent's house for 7 months straight 12 hours a day researching. I may have gotten in a meal a day, and if anyone came into my room I'd hurry them out so I could get back on the grind. After literally 7 months of very hard work – reading, watching videos, and engulfing myself completely into the craft – I stepped up my confidence level and was ready to begin. The only catch was that I had no money. I had quit my job as a personal trainer and moved home – I had nothing. I knew I had to get the money somehow, so I approached an investor and he gave me the capital to start up. Fast forward 16 months, and we just broke the £300,000 UK ($374,625) mark. To even say that to myself is absolutely crazy and now my focus is shifting to a desire to help others achieve this same level of success.

Ben: Chris, you've made over £300,000 UK, but to a lot of people this might seem out of reach. I want to clear up some limited beliefs here, because I think it's important to be honest from the beginning as to who can actually achieve the level of success that you've achieved. Who can do it?

Chris: I personally think that there are no limitations on the business model besides those that you impose on yourself. I see sellers on Amazon who are making millions every year, and to me that is overwhelming to those who are just starting out. £300,000 UK is a lot of money – I didn't set out to make that much, the cash just came. Once I set my processes up, everything just flows so well that you build up a ton of momentum where those revenue and sales factors just rise. Now, some people aren't committed to earning that much money. Maybe they just want financial freedom by doing this on the side while they work a part time job. Whatever the interest, wherever your passion lies, you can do that. If you want to turn this into a full time career, you can absolutely quit your 9-5 with this business model. It can be achieved at any revenue.

Ben: Absolutely! I think it's important to note that by focusing on a few very key things, anybody can find success in this business. So what are those crucial things that allow you to make money on Amazon while putting your business on autopilot to make you passive income while you sleep? The first is perfecting your Amazon listing from head to toe. Can you give some insight Chris?

Chris: Of course! When you search on Amazon for a product and you see all of the results, you are looking at product page listings. As a consumer, you are looking for the best product at the best price with a product listing that looks sharp visually and reads very well. As a seller, on the other hand, all you are going to notice is that there is a ton of competition. That's just the way it goes. Now, as a seller, you want to make your product page like your own website. This is the most crucial thing that you have to nail when creating your Amazon listing.

Look at it like your own canvas, where you can draw, pick points and perfect your Amazon listing. This listing consists of 4 major components: your title (the most important part of your listing), 5 key features (functions, visuals, benefits), images and description. You see a lot of product listings that are clunky and it's just a product page that you don't like to look at. The important thing, from a sellers point of view, is that if your product page looks and reads poorly, then it probably isn't going to convert. Again, you have to look at your product listing like a blank canvas where you dot your I's, cross your T's, and make sure that everything is of the highest quality you can manage to create.

Ben: If you have a product that is visually based – like a t-shirt or coffee mug – then you are competing against a massive number of other shirts and mugs. There are TONS of other options that consumers have out there. If you don't fully optimize your product page listing in order to stand out in the marketplace, you are going to get hammered by the competition. That being said, I want to analyze each of the 4 components of the perfect product page listing so that you, the reader, know exactly what you need to do to be successful.

Chris: Point number one, and it really is vital to standing out on Amazon's search engine. People search on Amazon for keywords, meaning they literally key (type) in words to the Amazon search bar in order to find items. Without keywords in your title, key features, description and backend keywords that are extremely relevant to your item (i.e. yoga mat for a yoga mat), you will not be putting your product in front of the millions of eyes that is the Amazon marketplace. So point one is to include 3 - 5 main keywords, both short tail (yoga mat) and long tail (yoga mat for beginners), in your product listing in all 4 spots – title, key features, description and backend keywords. You *must* include these keywords in the title of your product, as that is the most important determining factor for your Amazon visibility. However, these same keywords must be included in your key features and description at least once so that your listing has the potential to show up when those keywords are searched. Without these keywords in the various places mentioned, your listing will not be optimized and you will be missing out on all of the free traffic that Amazon sends your way. Picking these keywords is another beast, one that we will address later on.

Ben: Making sure that your product listing includes these keywords is important, but so is the actual writing of your key features and description. For best practices, it is crucial that you sell the benefits of your product in the key features and description. Don't just blandly tell the customer what they are going to get. Sell them on what they want!

Your title is what hooks them in and gets them interested so that by the time they are reading the key features and description you have a captive audience. Keep them engaged! You have to sell them the experience of the product by making them drool over it. Instead of simply informing, dazzle them! Make them question how they ever got along without the product. Once you've optimized the title, key features, and the description, you are on our way to perfecting the product page listing. However, there is one more element: the product images. Chris, how important is this piece of the puzzle and where should folks go to get high quality images?

Chris: This is another crucial part of making a killing on Amazon. If you don't have a good photo, nobody is going to click. I always refer back to YouTube; if you are searching around and you see a stellar video thumbnail, regardless of the title you are going to click it. That is just how it goes. Visuals are the way forward. It's like video in 2017 – I've heard that 90% of marketing and advertising will be video based. Related this to your product listing. Pick the photo that allows your product to stand out from the crowd. If everyone has a red image, pick a blue. If they are all showing passive shots, show an action. Do what you can to stand out. Now, Amazon has some guidelines as to how they want your product images to be. Your photo needs to be 1000 by 1000 pixels so it makes a nice centered, square image with the potential for a zoom factor. Whenever customers move their mouse over the product, they need to be able to zoom in and still see a crystal clear picture.

So where do you get these images? I'm not sure if my students are going to hate me for this, but I'm going to share it anyways because I want to provide as much value to you as possible. I go over to www.shutterstock.com to get photos. Let's say you are selling a phone cover, and you don't have the capital to bring in a professional photographer. What I would recommend is go over to Shutterstock, type in the keyword phone case, pick one of the stock images, and put the mockup file of your private label image onto the stock image. Your graphic designer should be able to do this easily regardless of the color, size or dimensions. To satisfy Amazon's guidelines, your images need to have a white background. The first image is more aimed at showing customers what the product is, with the next few demonstrating how to use it in action shots. For example, with the phone case the first photo would be with a white background, but the second could be a person talking on the phone with a scenic background. You could also do some promos and add them in on the visuals.

To recap, visuals are extremely important. Make sure you get very high quality images and you take advantage of every image slot available! Depending on whether you are selling in the US, UK, etc., you will have a certain limit to the number of images that you can upload. Make sure to use them all! Give your customers every possible reason to buy that you can. Take full advantage of every nook and cranny.

Ben: I want to jump in here for a second and backtrack. I'm assuming that some of the readers haven't even launched a single product on Amazon before. Chris mentioned having a graphic designer put the private label brand on the Shutterstock image. If I'm an average joe, however, I don't have any graphic designers on speed dial. Where do I find good graphic designers?

Chris: There are a few options here; you can go to Fiverr.com, Upwork.com, or my personal favorite Freelancer.com. These are outsourcing sites where you can post your project in full description and freelancers from around the world will start bidding on your project. You could potentially leverage your personal network on social media or put out some paid ads looking for people, but sites like those aforementioned make it extremely easy to find high quality freelancers that you can message one day and have a design the next. Especially when you are trying to save money in the beginning, establishing a long-term relationship with a designer on one of these sites can be a huge asset to your business.

When you are getting started, make sure to ask them a lot of questions: what are the prices? How long is it going to take? What experience do you have? Can I see previous projects you've done? Do not be afraid to ask questions! This goes for all areas of your life, not just business. The person who asks the most questions gets the most answers. The person who gets the most answers learns the most things. That's just the way it goes, so don't be afraid to ask questions!

Ben: Like you said, you can't be afraid to ask. You are the one who is hiring those freelancers. You are putting your money and resources on the line, so it is up to you to make sure you get the most bang for your buck. Don't just hire the first person that messages you about the job. I'd recommend getting a range of prices. Once you have been quoted by a minimum of 3 freelancers, you can then make an informed decision.

So at this point, we've covered optimizing your title, key features, description, images, and we've even thrown in some information on how to find a freelance graphic designer to be on your team. Next, we are going to discuss optimizing your Amazon Pay-Per-Click (PPC) to drive targeted traffic to your product listing.

Chris: PPC – Amazon has its own pay-per-click system that allows you to send traffic to your products. However, in order to take advantage of this system, you absolutely

MUST have your front end (what customers can see) optimized. If all of these aren't written properly with the optimization tips mentioned earlier, don't say PPC, don't think about it, don't click it, don't talk about it to a friend. Do NOT turn it on! You absolutely have to perfect your front end first. However, once you have optimized your front end, head over to the advertising section within your Seller Central Amazon account, and click that big fat button that says Amazon PPC.

From here you have two options. The first option you can turn is the automatic PPC Ad Campaign, where Amazon will gather and analyze all of the information in your front end – those sentences and phrases and all of the nitty gritty in your product page listing – and chuck it out to your customers. You want to set it up in such a way that you have all of your relevant keywords being targeted. From here, you can bid to have your ads shown for those different keywords. Because the Amazon advertising engine is based on an auction system, you must out-bid your competition for space to show your ads. That being said, the higher your competition in a certain market, the more you will have to pay per click in order to show your products.

In certain markets, you will have to pay a few dollars per click. Now, why would somebody pay that much per click (not per sale, but per click!)? The profit margin! With Amazon Private Label, you might be making $20-$30 per sale! If, and I know I keep coming back to this but it is this important, you have your product listing fully optimized and you can convert traffic into paying customers most of the time, then you can afford to pay a few dollars per click.

The last thing you have to do is set a daily budget, so I'm going to share with you a few tricks that you can put into your business here. I personally think that the higher daily budget you set, the higher Amazon will put you up in their search engine. Why? If you show Amazon that you are willing to drop some big bucks on your products, even if it doesn't always spend that much per day (sometimes it is organically capped by Amazon), it shows Amazon that you, as a seller, are a lot more serious about your products. Therefore, Amazon will be more inclined to chuck you up higher in the search rankings.

The second avenue with Amazon PPC is the manual budget. You've got your automatic campaigns running on all of the keywords you have on your page, but there might also be some keywords that didn't make the first cut but you still want to test. Cue manual PPC. This system is a great way to show Amazon that you want to be visible in different search terms, and that what the manual is for. Personally, I don't spend too much time or money on the manual budget. I'm a firm believer that if you have your product listing fully optimized, the automatic campaigns will be your highest converting marketing medium. When launching a product, I will typically spend about £234 and make back £1,464 in PPC. You can see the power that this system truly brings once you have your front end optimized completely.

Ben: Let's clarify a little bit. The biggest, most important thing here is to have your product page completely optimized. When people land on your product page, they buy. Once you've gotten your product page to convert, you then want to send as much targeted traffic as you possibly can that way.

Chris: You want to make your product page as stellar as you possibly can. When people land on it, you want them to say, "This is awesome. Regardless of how good this product is, I'm gonna buy it anyways because I want the experience of what this seller is offering me." Obviously you want your product to be of superior quality. In fact, if you don't have a high quality product, move on to something else. Many many sellers look past this most fundamental part of the Amazon selling process. They want their product on Amazon tomorrow, so they never look further into the long term. I would prefer to wait another 3 months to work out a high quality product with my supplier rather than chucking myself into the market with a subpar product and having to compete on price. When you have the same product as everyone else, you can't stand out on anything besides price.

Now, if you are going to put quality first, there are tons of ways to stand out: color, style, variations, packaging, patterns, boxing, there are endless ways to differentiate. Offer more value than anyone else in the market – the more value you can give to somebody in your market the better chances that they are going to buy your product. Do not go into a market if you aren't willing to differentiate, it's just not going to happen. It might seem to work in the short term, but who wants to only make money in the short term? No one. Look for that end goal in terms of selling your business. If you do the things we're telling you then you will be able to sell your business and retire in 3 – 5 years. That's the reality, and that's what I you to envision when you are starting out. Don't do this because you can make £30,000 or £40,000 or £100,000 a month, do this because in 3 – 5 years you can be set for a lifetime. Your family is taken care of. Your kids' kids are taken care of. That is the vision I set out with, and if you want to be successful in the long-term, then that's the vision that you need to have as well. Stop thinking short term and buckle down for the long term.

Ben: Just to be clear. If you follow the process that we are laying out for you here and follow it to the T, then in 3 – 5 years you can sell your Amazon FBA business and retire for life. I don't know of any other business model that is this directly headed to early retirement. If that isn't cool enough, you don't even have to sell your business if you don't want to! You can keep it going! Nothing is stopping you from reaching that £100,000 a month mark or higher, but having the option to retire in 3 – 5 years is powerful. But let's keep going.

We've talked about the product listing, including the title, key features, description and images (we even threw in a bit about finding freelancers), and we discussed Amazon PPC and making sure to have a long-term vision, let's talk about selecting the correct keywords for your products to show up on top of Amazon's search engine.

Chris: I personally think that this is the easiest thing to do with Amazon. Amazon is like Google, which is like YouTube; they are all powerful search engines even though Amazon is slowly moving past them in terms of volume. This is what makes it very easy and comfortable for us to search for these terms on Amazon and put that into our listing knowing that these search terms have massive potential. Here's how you do it. Let's say that we are trying to find keywords to sell a yoga mat. Go to the Amazon search bar and start typing in a few letters of the main keyword, yoga mat. Type in 'yo,' now stop. Look at the dropdown menu, the Amazon suggested searches, of what you've typed in. These keywords are what everyone is searching for on Amazon. These are the most powerful keywords that relates to these letters. Now type in 'g' and type in 'a' and type in a space. Look at all these results! This is how the keyword system works. This is one of the main ways that I do it.

But there's more. Type in yoga mat and press enter. Now, for this main keyword, you can see all of the top contenders and you can investigate them to see what's working. What keywords are they using? What is their title? What are their key features? What kinds of images do they have? You can put your binoculars on, have a sneak at their listings, and see what you can replicate/improve on. This is the system that everyone uses, but some people try to overcomplicate it. They look to Google for keywords, do all of these fancy things and get in their own way. Picking keywords is as simple as the steps I just mentioned. Practice it, put a smile on your face, and don't look too far into it!

Now, once you've mastered this system of picking your keywords, I want to share one more little secret that you can use when picking products. Google Trends. You can go over to Google trends, type in your main keyword, and Google will show you the volume and popularity of searches for that keyword over time. Keep in mind, I only use this if I'm unsure about a certain keyword. There are three different trends that you will probably see, growth, decline and maintenance. You want to see where this keyword is going by analyzing past trends. I always go for keywords that are very consistent, either they have been steadily growing over the past few years of they have been maintaining the same high volume/popularity over the past 5 years. Naturally you want to be patient with this process, but if you cross-reference your Amazon findings with Google Trends, you can just see if the keyword is going to pay off for you or not. Keep it simple. Do NOT overcomplicate this process or everything going on in your head will overwhelm you.

Ben: I want to help simplify this process a little more if possible. When picking keywords, you are just trying to figure out what your customers are typing into Amazon in order to find your products. Using the Amazon recommended search terms, you are picking the keywords that are the most relevant to your product. I have a secret for you too. In order to make sure your search results aren't being tailored to your account (Amazon is constantly collecting data on you), you want to be doing these searches in Incognito Mode (Chrome) or Private Mode (Safari). By being logged out of Amazon, you are getting what the majority of people see when they search. Then, take those keywords that you found on Amazon and double check them on Google Trends. This is a very logical, straightforward process. In order to find a yoga mat, people are going to type in "yoga mat!" It isn't rocket science! You don't want to fight it or try to use any tricks or shortcuts. Just utilize the process Chris and I have laid out for you in order to use Amazon to figure out Amazon.

Now Chris, let me ask you a question about your own personal preferences. Once you've done your research, you've picked your keywords and cross-checked with Google Trends, how do you know if you should change them?

Chris: This is simply a matter of letting your listing do it's thing. You don't want to focus too much attention worrying when you have a few bad days or a few good days, you have to look longer into the process. The only way to check which specific keywords are converting is through Amazon's internal PPC system. But again, don't focus too much on these little details. If you start running around frantically asking people a million questions and changing things here and there, you are going to end up back at square one.

Optimize your listing to its full potential, let it run its course, and if sales start coming in don't fight it! Don't change it to think "oh, if it's 8 sales I'm gonna change this little thing to get 10 sales." Be patient with this. Stay consistent. Do not add too many elements here or there, stay the course and focus in on that long-term vision. Once you start seeing success, start to scale up your PPC in a way that is viable financially. Don't rush into it. Set a low cost per click to start, set a medium daily budget, and then build from there. I think that the best way to do it is to measure the number of sales you are getting and the conversion rate of your PPC.

Ben: That is absolutely the best way to do it, and I have made the mistake of trying to change things too much instead of letting it run. It is not pretty, and you can never tell what is working and what isn't. Stay the course. That being said, there is still another crucial piece of the puzzle that we are going to discuss in this book: how to generate high quality, unbiased product reviews.

Chris: Okay, so I want to add some clarity to this because there has been a lot of confusion lately in the Amazon community. Before October 2016, you could, as a seller, go on to various websites and set your product for a discount. These websites had loads of reviewers that would write reviews for your product in order to get that discount. That ended because customers were getting mad at Amazon for biased product reviews, and even though it may seem more difficult to get reviews now, this new system is better for smaller business owners. Here's the thing. You can still give away products at a discount, but you have to do it properly. Amazon changed the rules to say that you can't give products in exchange for a review. That doesn't go to say that you can't set a discount code and have people purchase through that, especially on launch. Here's how you do it. You set the discount when you launch in order to spike the Amazon algorithm to get a low (better) Amazon Best Seller Rank and a better spot in the search rankings. This means that you could be sitting on page 100 in the first hour of your launch and at the end of the 24th hour of the day you could be on page 1 with the big players.

To get reviews, all you have to do then is email your customers that took advantage of the discount code and give them additional value using Amazon's internal messaging system. I would send them about 3 – 4 emails. The first would be congratulating them on their purchase and getting them excited about a free ebook that they would be getting in email two, so on and so forth. Then, in email three or four, thank them again for being a part of your company and write "if you would like to leave us some feedback, feel free to do so here" and include a link for them to leave a review. This is the best way to do it because you are incentivized to provide your customers with the utmost value and Amazon can see what you're doing (because it is done through their internal software).

Is this method more difficult to get reviews? Yes! For the long-term, however, is it going to be more valuable for you? Yes! Why do I say that? I look at it like this. Let's say I bring a phone cover (for example) to best-seller ranking. I've invested £5,000 and now I'm making 50 sales a day and have 100 reviews. Great! However, this means that a company with a £100,000 investment can come in and spend £25,000 getting reviews and I would be out of business. Amazon has seen that, and now bigger companies can't "buy-out" a market by selling so much product at a discount that the smaller businesses just can't compete. I truly believe that Amazon has seen that, and although people are getting frustrated in the short-term, I think this is the vision that Amazon is going with. This system is better than we can imagine because it really keeps the sellers' best interest at heart.

Ben: To simplify and summarize, basically what you want to do is give your customers a discount. You want to give them this discount during the launch of your product (the first 24 hours) in order to spike Amazon's algorithm because it is a mathematical algorithm and you want to give it what it needs. It needs sales, so you give it what it needs in order to put your product on page 1 for the keywords that you've picked earlier. Once you've made all of these sales, you want to follow up with your customers, and you want to give them more value. You want to thank them, provide them with more value, and turn them into lifetime customers. Then, you ask them for honest feedback. Not only will this strategy allow you to generate high quality, unbiased product reviews, but it will also give you a channel to truly listen to your customers and improve your product to suit their needs. These customers have voted for your product with their wallet, and they will tell you how you can improve. It is really that simple.

Let's recap. In order to make over $30,000 per month selling on Amazon, you need to understand and implement these four steps.

1. Perfect Your Amazon Listing From Head to Toe
2. Optimize Your Amazon Pay-Per-Click (PPC) to Drive Targeted Traffic to Your Product Listing

3. Select the Correct Keywords for Your Product to Show Up On Top of Amazon's Search Engine

4. Generate High Quality, Unbiased Product Reviews

Get on your grind and stay hustling. Financial freedom is NOT out of reach. Don't give up, and you will be rewarded for your efforts! Utilize what Chris and I have shared with you in this guide. Don't be afraid to read through it again and pick the pieces out that you need at the time you need it. The more knowledge you have about Amazon FBA the better.

The last piece of advice I have for you is to enjoy the journey. Not every path will end up where you thought would, and what you learn along the way may be worth more to you than the original goal. Failure is going to happen. Learn from it. The only way failure becomes permanent is if you let it. Stand up. Don't let anybody limit you or tell you that you can't do something. If you want it bad enough, anything is possible. Welcome to the game,

Amazon Seller.

Printed in Great Britain
by Amazon

24051326R00030